Waves Of a Woman

Vandana Prakash AKA Vandi

BookLeaf Publishing

India | USA | UK

Made with ❤ on the BookLeaf Publishing Platform
www.bookleafpub.in
www.bookleafpub.com

Dedication

This book is dedicated to my late grandmother, Roopavati Naidu, the woman who inspired me to be the woman today.

Acknowledgement

I would like to thank My Father for standing by me; My Mother for showing me the power of gratitude, awareness and forgiveness; My Brother for helping me to complete this journey.

A special thanks to my four angels – Sarah, Claudi, Odis, Ollie – who have been in my corner always.

Preface

'Waves Of a Woman' is a collection of poetry inspired by different experiences, moments and people who have crossed paths as well as been the core of my journey.

The complexity of the thoughts that have been portrayed through these poems is a culmination of the embodiment of us 'women'.

The hope is to dwell deeper into this experience and discover that we are bound by our identities woven into one tangent of who we are and the women we grow to become.

The Beginning

An infinite distance stretching into the
horizon
A glimmer runs across the waters whilst the
crashing of the waves
Tiny figurines sit alone, waiting and watching
To all their dreams once found and lost, they
stay latching

An envy of wonder, they stare with a soulful
need
A drop of hope, a little faith holding on for it
to take the lead
Tides grow stronger and pull away our only
desire
A connection yearned through any form we
aspire

An invisible layer, in sync like the birds that
fly carefree
Like the boundless ends and the everlasting
glory that encompasses the seas
Figurines are all we are and a purpose we
repeatedly try to seek

Extrinsic, we keep looking out instead of within

Our fight, our purpose, our lighthouse, our stories begin
The battle between darkness and light never seems to yield
Till we realise that it's the shadow, it's us that fate has sealed
The calmness only seeps the deeper we travel
Coz the waves crashing is only the start of our vessel.

Beautiful Surrender

The vibrancy seeps as my nightfall sets in
Like the tides that recede back, I reach out
within
Watching the colours make their way into
darkness
Memories I tucked away, starting to claw
their way up without a harness

Reaching its surface, I want to shrug off this
feeling
Only hoping it'll merge away like the clouds
thinning
Then slowly, in the distance, I peer through
the vacuum of stillness
Grasping onto anything, I hold onto the
invisible currents

Small lights I then see making its way through
from such a distance
The blanket that was drowning my sanity
slowly sways, letting through my innocence
Moments treasured like feathers into the
endless skies

With brightness with each one lighting up
like fireflies

Reminiscing in moments we can choose to
remember
I stay in the beauty of all my timeless
moments of beautiful surrender

Love

Years beyond, like the seas unknown
All the beautiful seeds I believe I sown
My Life with moments, you're always by my side
An emotion we move through variations of different tides

Love across the blue-green skies
Like a melody radiating through all earthly ties
Twirled and danced while the stars twinkled
Through the good and bad times that the universe sprinkled

The words unspoken I lay here in your awe
Your kindness and virtue, I believe it's the world's law
Your gentleness and the man you are
You make my heart wonder above and far

Rhythmic heart beats with yours and mine
A smile that you set into this unique gift of a kind

Seconds turn into minutes, where time
becomes relative
Thoughts like trees wavering in happiness
find their calmness

Serendipity surrounds me, engulfing me in
this joy of caress
Your voice, your stay, cowers my emptiness
The smile that never arose in such a long time
In the entirety of a day, you brought it back
to my music hymn

Thunderstorms in our midst I sit here beside
you
My feelings flutter like the butterflies that I'm
true
A whirlwind of emotions I feel overwhelmed
with a love so rare
My heart that pondered that got lost, you
hold close and care

A voice I lost and gained just when you stood
so still in front of me

A vessel empty and invisible you reached out
to finally see
Seasons passed and years did too, but in just a
moment
Ushered with all that's whole, an angel sense
of gift sent

Colourless memories turned into spectrums
of light
A fortune like the rainbow that turns up
when water and sun unite
Sweetness of ultimate cohesion settles
through me
And when my eyes meet, you shall see that's
very true

With you, I lay here in absolute serenity
A calmness so overwhelming that the world
stops spinning
Sit by my side, my darling, through every
sunrise and sunset
Let's see the world in its full glory and
I stay here mesmerised with you as my mate

A Girl's Curse

A wrinkled shirt with my hair tossed I only
ran to flee
Stood in a corner, in silence against the palm
tree
Voices behind me with fumes of alcohol in
the air
Barely could breathe and clutched on every
tear

Twelve years, they say, we become this
woman to be celebrated
We wait and think about the day when
metamorphosis is initiated
Wishing for a tiara or a wand that could make
us this beauty
Those thoughts, so innocent, shattered in
fifteen minutes of raw fury

Men with a familiarity of trust like hungry
wolves to their prey
I was overpowered in this situation with a
voice of no say

Eight years I wished across over shooting
stars, every plane that flies
To give me a shield, my person, who would
place me there in the highs

In the heavens of this world, hold my every
tear
Would make his forever with boundless love
and be a fighter for my fears
To the wolves, I went and blamed myself till
this day
The what ifs, so many, scenarios through time
with nothing to pray

Open my eyes and relive this, first of many
We are given the courage to isolate them,
blinding our sanity
The wait still stays, and now I'm thirty-four.
Living life solo is what we say but my secret
still lingers, tainting my core

Voices in the Night

Stories that travel through our minds play in
rewind like a stuck tape
Over and over again, we replay our every
move that could change our stakes
Blames that fall through like the voices in my
mind
Louder it resonates as I wake up to a
disconnected reality of a strange kind

To camouflage this hidden truth, I stay lying
in a form of paralysis
Powerless trying to fight the waves of this
unexplained emotion
Stuck in reverse gear, trying to change the
wheels of direction
Accepting every fear when the dangers posed
are very real

Tanked in a surplus of self-doubt, with unsure
ways forward
The darkness in my thoughts contouring my
gleaming sadness

Melancholy stands still like the sands that are
swept away
Tears too tired to weep; the spark that
glistened one day died in its make

The binds of history hold on as an extension
Glorified in its sinfulness, it lingers on with
its own stench
Pieces come apart like a puzzle I keep fixing
Time falls apart, a broken tape, a line with no
meaning

Truth be told, we have mummified every
emotion
The versions I create to protect oneself from
this grave self-destruction
The blank stare with outward disconnect
Flows on and on while the days pass on like a
star that shines long after its imminent death

Transit to happiness

Like a puppet in a frame, I string my limbs on
Showtime echoing in every direction I fix my
smile with a song
Take a breath just to settle the tears that
could flow through
Reminding myself of a reality that isn't my
truth

Catching on to little bubbles of happiness, I
tune in like the radio
Coz this is my song, my transit to happiness
to last till I can
A distant memory, the waves of uncontrolled
thoughts stay afar
Like a glass shielding the harshness I wait till
the doors slide in every hour

Moments that give me strength, warmth and
power, like inlay pearls and gifts
I gather from my audiences all the fallen
beautiful roses and their tips
Another persona I acclimate in no time –
that's the gift

Born with the strength to hold what stray to
my path with a lifeline lift

Toggling through characters of my own
written book
I soak in every role and play every puppet
that I, in time, took
Play the part, play it well, I tell myself
Hiding behind the stage, I direct and I do it
better with every take

The curtains close and like every other day,
performing with happiness, I close my eyes
The waves gush in and take me away to my
binding ties
Accepting the fate, I wait till tomorrow for
the curtains to rise
So my pearls, roses and tips keep me yearning
for those little highs

Companion

You made me believe in love at first sight
Your little paws, your big, beautiful eyes – we
instantly fell in love
You came close, your paws against my palm
I knew you were my love and will be forever
mine

My epitome of life, you sat beside me when
all things failed
Words unspoken I felt your cuddles and your
sweet fragrance
You pranced around when my tears flooded
down
Wiped away my fears in one glimpse and
upside frown

The world will never be complete when I had
to say goodbye
When you passed in my arms, it was the day I
finally wanted to die
You gasped your last breath in my arms and I
had to assure you I would be fine

With the sound of music, my Maria, my
Claudie you were always mine

It's time to let your soul go to join the stars in
the heavens above
My guardian angel, you were and will be in
the days ahead in my life
Not a day goes without you in my heart
With every blessing, I believe you were my
start

I still am a mom with siblings I now take care
They follow you and it's your essence that you
left that I see
I hear you on warning nights when it's wet
and cold
Your little bark near my pillow, the place you
always kept your hold

See you again, as I know it's you who will find
me
Leading my afterlife to its judgement and my
destiny

By The Sea of Thoughts

Through the sunset, there is a glimpse of the
never-before
A journey I started with myself, the person
who I came to be
Besides this, spans the waves turning into
tides
All the woven stories into wound-out hives

Untangled like weaves of time, this moment
stays untethered
Here I am with a soul like no other
Within an unknown journey, almost like a
seam that's worn
The heart stays still in a moment of the
ending

With the music around us, we can hear each
other sing
Solitude within a journey we reward this time
Like two souls that found their way to a view
that almost feels like endless miles

Let's stay idle with all that surrounds our pain
joy and sorrow

Reminiscing every drop like it's our way
within
Conversations seem to flow like the sunset
peering through the clouded crux
Resonance-like reason passes like an innate
flux
Untampered filters we cave into our versions
we found

The seas, the journeys, like the stories untold
I find the unfettered battles being again born
Lay here above through this beautiful crest
The beams that lead finally find their nest

Time stands still in the past
A phase that seems like a recurring wave
Against the tide, you feel like beating it
rather than acceptance
It's a part of your journey that lingers on

Holding on to the trauma that are bricks
built into a wall

It's one step at a time hearing that faint voice
of a call
A sense of power you pass on from your past
to your present
The grit that stays alive, a spark that builds on
your untamed flame

That will, that strays away at home, blurry
through these net of notions
Forgiveness is the only way out; it's your own
innate potion
A second replaces a minute to let go
To realise that you are complete like the seeds
that grow

Deep-rooted memories can make a coven of
safety
Coz you hold the power to hold on to the
horizon, which only you can see
And gratitude will set onto you like the
sunset to this sunset
An overwhelming feeling of freedom, you will
fight for what's best

Love and Violence

You bring me close and then push me away
Show me the rainbows and dark stormy
waves
I wish to believe you when we are in this
purgatory sense
Caressing me with kindness, you seem to
know me well

Silencing the pain and covering my bruises
Watching myself in the mirror of shame of
losses,
I wish for a better day waiting for the cycle to
end
No one around to call out for; it can be only
God-sent

In something I did, you pushed to shove
My hair tangled in your watch I try to get
away
My feet caught at a wedge; I struggle to
balance

And the look in your eyes turns from red to
grey

You say you're sorry that it was a mistake
You pull me close and I push you away
The eyes turn red with anguish I now know
Unstoppable you will be if I don't move from
your webbed cove

Vows with promises of no harm in my way
Taken to the moment, it suddenly was three
years back in May
Through sickness and health, you worded to
be by my side
Lows and highs, you said you would be my
ship and my everlasting stride

A glance through back in time, I was walking
towards you
With a smile of happiness and joy of our
celebration in eternity and virtue
Questions how we are now stay unphased in a
stillness of sorrow
I gave you my heart and you gave me mine to
borrow

With a hope that tomorrow will be a better
day
I lay in a corner, wishing for the sun's rays to
make their way
A glimpse of us looking at each other on the
day we unite
Gives me a calm and finally, I close my eyes

My Unborn

As I close my eyes in the bleak of night
Your image becomes clear within my sight
Stretch out my arms, bringing you close to
my chest
You lay with your little arms and feet tucked
against me in our little nest

I hummm away into this mystical feeling
Lost in your gaze, my bright-eyed beauty as
you see the ceiling
Your little fingers into my palm I hold on
gently
Your smell radiates like the freshness of
violets tethered

Stories of how I wish I could fight for you
Started fairy tales that got weary coz a broken
home is not what I wanted you to grow up in
Keep waiting to bring you to this world so I
can envelope you in my bubble of love
A wait that's taking forever, a wait I don't
know how far along

A promise with prayers to bring beauty to
this world
Devoid of the fog settling, I see growing like a
mould
Yes, a true fear of what you might have to go
through
I know you will have a heart of gold much
more than your mother's truth

A tear makes its way onto an empty
pillowcase
The image fades away, saying goodbye
Eyes slowly close in, waiting for tomorrow's
night to settle through
My unborn, you are my angel; you will be my
dream coming true

Darling the letters I write of the world are for
you to live
Shine bright and grow your wings as wide as
you can
You are my one, only love that will heal the
hearts of many

The time of wait will end as your purpose is
destined

24

Expectation

A storm that's been brewing for years,
patience lacking, I never hear myself out
The world with its expectations keeps
trudging onto this non-stop expressway
Where a detour is considered formidable,
But failing to listen has coated me more than
was fathomable

Strength misunderstood, we battle within
and wait for time to matter
Every moment that blocks our sanity is the
way we climb our depths of darkness
Words spoken in less than a few to oneself
Moments captured; it's a beginning with the
untampered truth

An identity, a form and shape to look into the
mirror of acceptance
Facing a conflict unexplained and unmatched,
a fight, a mission with a sense
Driven by variables that are uncontrolled, yet
we hold onto

Pressured into factors determined by innate
factors of one being

Mapping our mind to create responses and
like pieces of a puzzle
Not knowing the result of its very being, the
end of this fortune wheel
Struggle of darkness, seats in the loneliness
we feel
Not knowing the way forward in the cycle of
one to heal

Scarred with the past, with shackles to our
feet
One step forward and one step behind, stuck
in the past so deep
Let go, they say, forgive we must, move on
with hope
And the universe will bring all things good so
we can cope

Simple and yet so complex, the journey never
ends
Wounds that healed, yet the scars remain

Reality-devoid, we keep trying to make sense
of our wars
Like blisters that arise, we try tending to our
soars

No answer, nor a question; we can never hold
close
Just the comfort that the struggle is real and
for most
You are not alone and you're going to be okay
With one step forward, we can assure each
other in this way

A Woman

An embodiment of everything beautiful
seated at the door of heaven
Tales of musicians, arts folk, nurturers and
gatherers – an infinite beacon
Takes spread to lands far and wide across the
seas of seven skies
The stars that glitter in the bed of
untampered beauty in which it lies

Have a heart at the centre and make history
with her existential tenure
She comes in forms of nature, inventions,
inspirations and explorations
Millenniums have seen this in repetitive
consciousness
Unexplored territory for the many, we still
remain a mystery

The ability to love even with science
undefined
Creates life with a soul for which only God is
known to possess

A warrior, a mentor, a lover, a prayer, a carer,
a forgiver with only a few I quote
In a world of many, she takes forms and
moves gracefully like the breeze through time

The wonder of a woman
The wonder of the ninth
The one always present
Yet forgotten in plain sight

The woman I chose to be
The woman, she shares her soul with me
Journeys different and stories so wide apart
But bound by our countless expanses, we are
engraved in this ground forever

Vulnerabilities Spoken

Lives spent in silence of what was said
Lie in the mystery of how things could have
changed yet
Passing clouds, we meet people we never
know for how long
Brings us sunshine, rain and our emotions like
a storm

The fear of loss engrains our DNA with life
and love
Trying to weed it out, we pull ourselves away
from this very now
Anticipation of the unknown is like
breathing in a vacuum
Space all around and the heaviness sits on our
chests like a dark loom

Paralysed by its expanding presence, we are
forced to lay still
Thoughts of our hauntings move around with
no place to hide
Gasping for air, we reach for downward
further

And realise we are alone in this battle with
fear

Paths untaken and journeys that lost their
ways
Once so sure, doubt engulfs us in this
unsolvable maze
Tamed and trained, we do what we've been
told
A lie we are living and eventually cards dealt,
we fold

Like a drop with no end, breath is only left
Like space around us but stuck in a crest
Like a canvas with no colour to paint
Like a gravestone set in and nameless, it
stands

Soothe your soul now that the worst is
already here
Bit by bit, one guiding light can steer our
path clear

It's time to break the shackles that held onto
us
It's our time to pick up our pieces and move
to the next

Travels log

Nervous and anxious, I find myself on a
one-way ticket
Not knowing what the universe has in store
for this time I set
Unfamiliar spaces, people I encounter right
from the start
I hide my shyness and breathe, starting with a
'hi' from my heart

A yes, no maybe of acceptance, I plunge
With no going back, I wait for a reply
A smile of warmth, I look at you and ask
where you are from
Intrigued by the courage you take, a leap of
faith, we found each other

Instant connection, my destiny had spoken
A trust in the universe reaffirmed, which was
once broken
A bond so immediate beyond this moment
that it led
With just a smile, we exchanged a few words
and our journey – a bridge in sand – it set

A bridge of our life with absolutely nothing
to hide
Calming and soft like the oven's warmth and
gentle tide
Spent hours that were little capsules of
happiness
Felt like the world stood and shared thoughts
that were limitless.

Charisma and charm endowed in all the
evenings that we shared
Loving every moment you become a person, I
really cared
Life with its untold curves and speed bumps
that it throws
Little joys and stories heard through in the
days to come, you protect me from the lows

Bonds that are created in glimpses of the
goodness that exists
Affirmation of positivity, the best therapy in
a form
Grows the unknown hopes that I once gave
up and lost

Like a fire that burned bright, the cruelty had
a great cost

People in their truest form, like an interim
gift the universe bestows
Open one's eyes to absorb the whole
experience it shows
Adventures of many become like lucky
charms I wear
Every person, with their humanity and the
stories we share

Unmasked and open to the truth, I see myself,
a future heir
A struggle of identity and loss feels like a blip
and nothing more I see
When the going gets hard, I channelise these
trinkets when I fall to my knee
We sometimes struggle and get stuck in our
quicksands of pain
Failing to see we are tethered together like
life support and never in vain
I sit here, lying in awe most times
When silence surrounds me a peace, just a
tune of wind chimes

Gratitude overwhelming; I'm blessed to this
day
Coz with all your little hearts I borrowed and
hold close to stay
A smile in silence, with the emptiness filling
up
I want to thank each one of you for my
journey this far

Mother

The lushness and rush of these valleys you
create
With hills of music and mountains of
beautiful surrender
Creations so unique, a gift unconditional
Expectations, a word invisible to its meaning

You keep giving and giving in a cycle that
never ends
Healing in your sight is like reaching beyond
our sense
A true inspiration surrounds us in the chaos
that exists
The spectrums of colour you once shined
clear but now manmade mists

I feel your pain sometimes when your fury
hits your own
The love you must feel, the betrayal that we
have repeatedly shown
Your canvas with unmatched beauty engulfs
us in an untold vastness

Filling this world with the blanket of wonder
protecting us from our darkness

The skies of shades take form when you awake
The feeling of change, like your emotions at
stake
Mustered by your artistry, you are truly an
everlasting shine
Lived with us from the beginning of every
beautiful kind

I bow down to you and respect every creation
Faith you keep showing in a hope that is our
evolution
Humanity is all you pray for our hearts to
grow
Seeds you continue to grain these lands and
the ceaseless love you show

A Beautiful Day

When my lover became my friend one day
The rainbows stretched over these skies, I lay
In a sense of serenity, I felt complete and
whole
The one I thought was obsolete started
beating on its own

The tunes become music notes that I could
feel
Every little detail so clear that my senses
started to heal
An inside smile finally peering through these
eyes
A subtle and yet strong feeling, like the
high-flying kites

We travel and look for this unspoken bond of
sorts
But showing to the world needless to say I can
handle things on my own
Yearn for belongingness I witness this
transformation

Of how I just switched on when you bought a
light of your own

Time is relative and a chapter I can't foresee
But this moment I lay with you, a moment
with me
Silence becomes music, and my eyes are only
smiles I can't speak
Coz it's the feeling that hums its way taking
me to my existence, my peak
Happiness is not forever, we say
But for now, let me enjoy this very day

A Distant Lover

A table so quiet and empty with plates set in
squares
I wait for every little sound, hoping you are
making your way through the stairs
Hours I wait to listen to all the pieces of your
day
A painting rests on the wall with I love you
words you used to say

The last sun ray hits the plate that glows in
fabrics of colour
And your reassurance once that made every
meal
Is now reduced to an empty chair
Your eyes brown so deep and gentle

Your gaze so calm and soft, made this world
so simple
I yearn for those days back again, a prayer I
know even the gods can't say
Like the Van Gogh we once spoke about
A language between seas you once learnt
about

Cultures so different you set your feet next to
mine
We made a lifetime of memories in a space so
undefined
My mind capturing every little movement,
how you swayed with me
In a time when time stood very still

Expressing my little pleasures, you listened to
me talk away
My world met with colours I never knew
existed other than this mundane grey
You will read this miles across the oceans with
stars we both will see
Just know you are my heartbeat and will keep
my key

Hoping your steps come closer to mine on the
same plane our dreams become one
The tunes of chimes create tones of the open
winds and finally, I see you
Moving with the same beautiful beat
Capturing a future just to be wanted and
known

Close my eyes to this beauty I settle in to
meet you in our dreams

Birth and Death

Born into a world, our innocence we enter
this stage
Profound with hope and dreams that fill our
eyes
Untouched with the shades of our unforeseen
journey
Unknown ways, unturned movement of tides

Day by day, a little step at a time forgone of
expectations
Seeing life from a third view, spectate from a
high-raised platform
The adult that now I have become, like scenes
played over again
Makes me ponder on the times I said goodbye

The hardest part witnessing our own strides
and low depths
Like the canyon with its enigma and yet
dangerous trenches
Is our lives that wander on through crevices
so deep

Every stream, every path meandering, taking
its own leap

Tugged with each other every narrow
pathway with glimmers of sun rays
Come together into one stream of constant
highway
Like the treads that wove us, every experience
interwoven
Creating layers over our soul that become our
sole coven

Emotions of pain and joy like a binary coding
Embeds into our human beings and their very
existence
Vulnerabilities of reaction to our moments
that gather
Like a mirror I stare, trying to overcome this
tether

Simplicity is my journey I strive to reach
So when death comes knocking
The birth cycle will finally complete
My eyes lay to rest with the treads now
disappearing

The ashes I simply become going back to the
land I came from

46

Loneliness Amongst Lovers

Loneliness sets in even with you by my side
A beginning so vibrant like the beauty of
wilderness
With so many spoken emotions, the days
became nights by the ocean
Never seemed enough while time was
non-existent

With a yearning for awe and wonder, I sat
there
Our journey so promising I knew this was it
Days became months and years felt like a
standstill
You are now here but we stand alone together

Barely hanging on with this undone tether
Unwilling to reach out even an inch to the
right
We look away with steps that were once in
sync together
Frustration, irritation and anguish of blame
With hurtful words putting each other to
shame

When did the weed start to grow so wild
Poisoning the beauty of our bond, which was
untainted
Now all I see are the reasons I am once again
alone
You reminded me once that this day would
never be shown

But here we are, from friends to lovers to
family
And back to strangers, we walk side by side
Nothing inside, like an empty puppet with
only strings with no soul

Loud Silence

Scenarios of every moment we shared
Times when you showed me you cared
Moments of joy expressed in every form
You pulled down the wall, years I took with
every storm

And one day, when I was the closest to let you
in
You held me against my own, saying it was my
fault
Times that I misread run like a series of
mishaps
My want to believe in the idea of you shot me
down

Confidence in reading people, you managed
to put away my crown
Question and self-doubt overtook every
decision
That's the moment I knew this was a
new-found betrayal
Loyalties I believed to have faith in with a
leap of faith

Now all I see in the mirror is a reflection of
my wraith

The journey of self-heal begins once more
As I cry in silence with the burden of pain in
my own narrative lore

Leading Light

Roads beyond the control of the weave of life
Tangled through bridges of the hurt of knives
Horizons untouched, we scream to reach
Our epitome of self we would want to give

We hide in the shadows society trolled
Every morning, every one minute somehow
we withhold
If only diversity humanity, we bring our
doubt to faith
Could we extinguish these thoughts that
make our fate?

For most loving thoughts, the shields of
acceptance
I pledge and kneel that your essence brings
character
Time passes and we seem to blame
Every version, every essence that is redundant
to the sane

Find yourself and hold this tight

Coz tomorrow will always be your fight to
the infinite
When I caved in to everything known
I met you in the fondest way

A wave of emotion that I can't comprehend
And a soul that can barely feel it's end
You came like a light in these withered nights
Like a glimpse of my only lamp, shining
bright

We walked miles like time never has known
Our existence, like life's music and its tone
Your smile sways every moment from start to
night
And your absence creates a void in every sight

Moments I relive and remember
You are now my special person, my one to
always tender

Broken tides

When I have to leave you with my arms
wrapped
I have my reality gush in like a universe that
has been warped
Waking into you, I push myself away from
having this feeling
Surrendering to an unknown entity, I find
myself kneeling

I fight my urge to feel these emotions and
words unsaid
Submerged into the depths of my detachment
from all who I cared
Asked many times how I manage my smile
with sorrow
I keep telling life that maybe I never need
more

The pain is real but the scars are invisible
Like a victim of self-harm, I hide it with
thoughts of self-kill
All I say through my eyes of masked
expectations

Come closer and ask you thee to read
between my hymns

54

Numbness, a feeling I trained in the years
that I lived
Passed by every moment on drugs so livid
Painful joy I call it in one
After all, I'm not a soul but just the universe's
toy

Healer

Like a shooting star, the rarity of your arrival
With wishes that I did, you came with my call
When I lost my way and roamed without
hope
You arrived from the skies, teaching me how
to cope

Only like a chapter that comes to an end, I
know
Like quicksand, I felt stuck and your hand
came through
Pulled me with the strength I lacked like a
purposeless body
Brought me to the solidity of my reality with
a tinge of honesty

The power that you emit vibrates like my rush
of adrenalin
Washing away all that's past, my trauma and
my sins
Carrying me through steps I couldn't find
myself pacing

Walked with the burden of my past
protecting my heart in its casing

56

I looked right at you when the noise
submerged into calm
In my life, a security of sorts finally kept me
from the world's harm
Saved me and salvation, you found me
My dear friend, you lay here with sight,
finally that I see

Beyond

Years beyond, like the seas unknown
All the beautiful seeds I believe are sown
My life, the moments, you always are by my
side.
An emotion, we move through different tides

Red sands like my heart, I bleed
Through the grains I see, I heed
Love across the blue-green skies
Like a melody through earthly ties

Like the skies asked why
And you answered with a cry
An answer which you never lied about
I never thought out loud

Here we are at the moment to beckon
And I believe we'd be alright, I reckon
Forever in this dance, remember we pranced
Twirled and tingled while the stars twinkled.
Good and bad times that the universe
sprinkled

Made time when it was needed, never was it
pleaded
All you needed was a smile; you hadn't seen it
in a while
These beautiful skies I found – believe me,
we'd fly unbound
We are in harmony together, like the waves as
one

Yes, darling, we see these horizons through all
the skies
And no high mountains or low valleys will
ever find our grace
So let's say our prayer that reaches me
through the crucifix
And admire god's creation above the window
The universe unbound and beautiful in
stillness

The Perfect Storm

In circles, we travel where corners cease
Struggles that seem like a never-ending loop
Sanity coming and going, trying to get a new
knife's lease
Our very own damaged thoughts making a
coup

Around ourselves, we bury our self in a
bottomless moat
Clutching for an instinct for survival of sorts
Naked and bruised, hoping for kindness in a
coat
Judgements and layers of insecurities
drowning with a heavy cost

Tossed like the storms that we sense around
Peering into the skies, we are in the eye of
this hurricane.
Bits of skin peeled off with the first wave of
destruction
I only can breathe, awaiting the upcoming
detriment

Free falling into this pit of the past
Scars over scars the pain so still with my
breath coming to it's last
Images of surrender with the thought of
letting go is now clear
Swallowing the tablets by the side table I lay
for it to end

Choking on the physical body engulfs me
with a calmness
It's over and it finally ended the battle of life
is a faraway thought
Floating away, the clouds finally pick me up
The innocence as light as a feather can fly
away till this stops

9 789363 304512